Mexican Ice-cream

&

Paletas

Homemade Ice-cream Recipes

Maria Gomez

2018

Copyright @2018 By *Maria Gomez*

All Rights Reserved.

The following book is reproduced below with the goal of providing information that is as accurate and as reliable as possible. Regardless, purchasing this book can be seen as consent to the fact that both the publisher and the author are not responsible for your personal coverage, and that any recommendations or suggestions made herein are for reference purposes only. Professionals should be consulted as needed before undertaking any of the action endorsed herein.

This declaration is deemed fair and valid by both the American Bar Association and the Committee of Publishers Association and is legally binding throughout the United States.

THIS BUNDLE INCLUDES THE FOLLOWING BOOKS:

[25 Mexican Ice Cream and Sorbets Recipes](#)

[PALETAS: Top 20 Mexican Ice Pops](#)

Table of Contents

25 Mexican Ice Cream and Sorbets Recipes 6

Ángel Negro Ice Cream 8

Balsámico Strawberry Ice Cream............... 10

Curaçao and Tequila Sorbet............... 12

Golden Passion Fruit Ice Cream 14

Delicate Blaze Ice Cream............... 16

Hot Picante Ice Cream 18

Mamey Sapote Ice Cream 20

Pineapple, Peppermint, and Mango Ice-cream 22

Pulque Liquor Berries Ice cream............... 24

Rose Petals Sorbet............... 26

Açaí Berry Ice Cream............... 28

Anejo Cuatro Chocolate Ice Cream 30

Avocado Ice Cream with Spicy Chocolate Syrup............... 32

Banana and Cacahuates Ice Cream 34

Fresita Strawberry Ice Cream 36

Ice Cream de Chantilly and Raspberry 38

Mexican Horchata de Arroz Ice Cream 40

Nances and Apricot Ice Cream 42

Passion Fruit Ice Cream 44

Pineapple Arbequina Sorbet............... 46

Ruddy Reposado Ice Cream............... 48

Sapodilla de Veracruz Ice Cream............... 50

Tropical Mamoncillo Sorbet 52

Tropical Mango and Cantaloupe Ice cream 54

Vanilla and Gold Tequila Ice Cream 56

PALETAS: Top 20 Mexican Ice Pops.. 59

"Boozy" Apple - Cherry Ice Popsicles 63

Agua de Jamaica and Cantaloupe Ice Pops 65

Cachaça Banana and Raspberry Popsicles 67

Cayenne Mango Popsicles 69

Coconut and Chocolate Bounty Ice Pops 71

Creamy Lemon Popsicles with Rosemary 73

Creme de Banana and Almonds Pops 75

Dulce de Leche and Salted Coco Syrup Pops 77

Frozen Mexican Wine Popsicles 79

Hot Cinnamon Cucumber Popsicles 81

Jicaleta and Tequila Liqueur Popsicles 83

Nutty Vanilla Popsicles 85

Quirky Guanábana Popsicles 87

Rumy Mamey Sapote Popsicles 89

Sour Guanabana Blueberry Popsicles 91

Sparkling Champagne Berry Popsicles 93

Spicy Mango and Chamoy Popsicles 95

Strawberry and Xtabentún Popsicles 97

Stunt Popsicles with Passion Fruit Cream 99

Tarragon Avocado Popsicles.. 101

25 Mexican Ice Cream and Sorbets Recipes

Did you know that...?

- The original name of Mexico was Tenochtitlan an Ancient capital of the Aztec empire.
- Mexico has around 117 million people according to the population census 2012.
- The official name of for Mexico is the United Mexican States
- Mexico is the most famous for its tequila, which is made from agave cactus.

Ángel Negro Ice Cream

Servings: 8

Preparation Time: 25 minutes

Nutrition Facts

Serving size: 1/8 of a recipe (3.4 ounces)

Percent daily values based on the Reference Daily Intake (RDI) for a 2000 calorie diet.

Nutrition information calculated from recipe ingredients.

Amount Per Serving

Calories 363.71

Calories From Fat (57%) 208.13

% Daily Value

Total Fat 24.1g 37%

Saturated Fat 14.26g 71%

Cholesterol 151.45mg 50%

Sodium 23.25mg <1%

Potassium 44.32mg 1%

Total Carbohydrates 37.8g 13%

Fiber 1.1g 4%

Sugar 25g

Protein 3g 6%

Ingredients

5 oz dark chocolate 60 - 80% of cocoa solids, chopped

3 cups whipped cream

4 egg yolks

1 cup sugar

2 Tbs Mexican red wine (Nebbiolo, Dolcetto or Barbera)

Instructions

1. Place chopped chocolate in a microwave-safe bowl.
2. Heat for 30 seconds; remove the bowl from the microwave and stir.
3. Set aside to cool down.
4. Repeat heating for 15 to 20 seconds, stirring between, until the chocolate is completely melted.
5. Whisk the egg yolks and sugar with a fork (or electric mixer) until a thick mixture is obtained.
6. Add melted chocolate and continue to stir.
7. Add the cooking cream and pour the wine stir slightly.
8. Place the ice cream mixture in a large container, put it in the freezer for 4 hours or more.
9. Remove the ice cream mixture from the freeze, place in a bowl and with the help of electric mixer beat for 2-3 minutes.
10. Place the container back in the freezer for 6 hours.
11. Repeat the process at least 4 times to break up the ice crystals.
12. Let the ice cream at room temperature 15 minutes before serving.

Balsámico Strawberry Ice Cream

Servings: 8

Preparation Time: 40 minutes

Inactive Time: 1 hour

Nutrition Facts

Serving size: 1/8 of a recipe (3.8 ounces)

Percent daily values based on the Reference Daily Intake (RDI) for a 2000 calorie diet.

Nutrition information calculated from recipe ingredients.

Amount Per Serving

Calories 176.15

Calories From Fat (42%) 74.04

% Daily Value

Total Fat 8.43g 13%

Saturated Fat 5.15g 26%

Cholesterol 30.57mg 10%

Sodium 10.33mg <1%

Potassium 141.21mg 4%

Total Carbohydrates 25.86g 9%

Fiber 1.14g 5%

Sugar 23g

Protein 0.84g 2%

Ingredients

1 lb strawberries

3/4 cup date palm sugar

1 tsp balsamic vinegar

3/4 cup cream

1 tsp molasses

1/2 tsp cornstarch

1 tsp pure vanilla extract

Instructions

1. Combine and stir the strawberries, date sugar and the balsamic vinegar in a bowl.
2. Place it in the refrigerator for one hour.
3. Beat the cream with the help of electric mixer on high until the cream reaches stiff peaks.
4. Add the strawberries, molasses, cornstarch and vanilla extract; beat for 2 minutes.
5. Place the ice cream mixture in a freezer-safe container with the lid, and freeze the ice cream in the freezer for 4 hours.
6. Transfer frozen mixture to a bowl and beat with a mixer until smooth.
7. Repeat the process at least 5 times to break up the ice crystals.
8. If your ice cream gets too firm in the freezer, allow it to thaw at room temperature for 15-20 minutes before serving.
9. Enjoy!

Curaçao and Tequila Sorbet

Servings: 6

Preparation Time: 10 minutes

Nutrition Facts

Serving size: 1/6 of a recipe (6.5 ounces).

Percent daily values based on the Reference Daily Intake (RDI) for a 2000 calorie diet.

Nutrition information calculated from recipe ingredients.

Amount Per Serving

Calories 173.58

Calories From Fat (0%) 0.6

% Daily Value

Total Fat 0.07g <1%

Saturated Fat 0.01g <1%

Cholesterol 0mg 0%

Sodium 70.2mg 3%

Potassium 41.86mg 1%

Total Carbohydrates 11.27g 4%

Fiber 0.17g <1%

Sugar 0.63g

Protein 1.3g 3%

Ingredients

2 1/3 cups of water

1/2 cup of lemon juice

3/4 cup of orange flavored Curaçao liqueur

2/3 cup of Tequila

2 egg whites

Lemon slices and salt for decoration

Instructions

1. Place water, lemon juice, Curaçao liqueur and Tequila in your high-speed blender.
2. Blend for 30 seconds and pour in a freezer-safe container with a lid, and freeze for 4 hours.
3. Beat the egg whites until frothy.
4. Add frozen mixture to egg whites in your high-speed blender (*check if your blender handles frozen things well), and blend for 60 seconds.
5. Place again in a freezer and freeze for 4 hours. Serve in chilled champagne decorated with a lemon and salt border.

Golden Passion Fruit Ice Cream

Servings: 10

Preparation Time: 20 minutes

Nutrition Facts

Serving size: 1/10 of a recipe (3.7 ounces)

Percent daily values based on the Reference Daily Intake (RDI) for a 2000 calorie diet.

Nutrition information calculated from recipe ingredients.

Amount Per Serving

Calories 117.9

Calories From Fat (1%) 0.79

% Daily Value

Total Fat 0.09g <1%

Saturated Fat 0.01g <1%

Cholesterol 0mg 0%

Sodium 14.53mg <1%

Potassium 201.36mg 6%

Total Carbohydrates 29.55g 10%

Fiber 0.16g <1%

Sugar 28.79g

Protein 1.11g 2%

Ingredients

1 cup of fresh orange juice

2 Tbs lemon juice

1 cup of sugar

2 cups of fresh Golden passionfruit pulp

2 large egg whites, beaten

Instructions

2. Heat the orange and lemon juice with sugar in a saucepan over medium-high heat; stir until sugar is dissolved completely.
3. Add the Golden passion fruit pulp (granadilla) pulp, stir well and chill in the fridge.
4. Freeze the mixture for two hours and then add the stiffly beaten egg whites and then freeze again.
5. Transfer frozen mixture to a bowl and beat with a mixer until smooth.
6. Repeat the process at least 5 times.
7. This will to avoid ice cream crystallization.
8. Serve and enjoy!!

Author Notes

Granadilla is the Spanish word for passion fruit and often refers specifically to the fruit of Passiflora ligularis.

Delicate Blaze Ice Cream

Servings: 10

Preparation Time: 15 minutes

Inactive Time: 6 hours and 15 minutes

Nutrition Facts

Serving size: 1/10 of a recipe (4 ounces)

Percent daily values based on the Reference Daily Intake (RDI) for a 2000 calorie diet.

Nutrition information calculated from recipe ingredients.

Amount Per Serving

Calories 333.5

Calories From Fat (68%) 225.58

% Daily Value

Total Fat 25.83g 40%

Saturated Fat 14g 70%

Cholesterol 65mg 22%

Sodium 277.11mg 12%

Potassium 135mg 4%

Total Carbohydrates 23.22g 8%

Fiber 0.05g <1%

Sugar 21.77g

Protein 3.89g 8%

Ingredients

2 cups cream cheese

1 cup granulated sugar

1 tsp salt

1 cup sour cream

3 cup Mascarpone cheese

1 cup coconut milk

2 tsp pure vanilla extract

1/4 cup Tabasco hot sauce, to taste

Instructions

1. Beat the cream cheese in a food processor or in a high-speed blender until soft.
2. Add the sugar, salt and sour cream and blend until smooth and creamy.
3. Add the Mascarpone cheese and continue to blend for further 10 - 15 seconds.
4. Pour the coconut milk and vanilla and blend until well incorporated.
5. If you use the ice cream machine, follow the manufacturer's instructions.
6. Otherwise, empty the mixture in a freezer-safe container (with a lid over).
7. Freeze for at least 6 hours.
8. Transfer frozen mixture to a bowl and beat with a mixer until smooth. Repeat the process at least 4 times.
9. This will to avoid ice cream crystallization.
10. Let the ice cream at room temperature for 15-20 minutes before serving.
11. Spread the Tabasco sauce on a platter and place the ice cream balls; serve.

Hot Picante Ice Cream

Servings: 6

Preparation Time: 30 minutes

Nutrition Facts

Serving size: 1/6 of a recipe (3.3 ounces)

Percent daily values based on the Reference Daily Intake (RDI) for a 2000 calorie diet.

Nutrition information calculated from recipe ingredients.

Amount Per Serving

Calories 299.08

Calories From Fat (40%) 119.8

% Daily Value

Total Fat 13.79g 21%

Saturated Fat 8.61g 43%

Cholesterol 41.11mg 14%

Sodium 124.13mg 5%

Potassium 203.81mg 6%

Total Carbohydrates 41.55g 14%

Fiber 0.37g 1%

Sugar 36g

Protein 4.56g 9%

Ingredients

1 cup condensed milk

2 Tbs fresh butter

1/4 cup sugar

3 Tbs boiling water

1 Tbs cornstarch

2 Tbs water

1/4 cup cream

2.6 oz dark chocolate, melted

1 tsp Instant coffee

hot sauce to taste (Valentina Salsa Picante, Texas Pete, Tapatio)

1 pinch of salt

Instructions

1. Combine the condensed milk, butter and sugar in a container.
2. Pour the boiling water and stir until all ingredients combine well.
3. In a small cup dissolve a cornstarch with water, and add to milk mixture.
4. Add the milk cream and give a good stir.
5. Chop the chocolate and place in a microwave safe bowl for 2 minutes on 50%.
6. Remove from microwave and stir 2 - 3 times.
7. Add melted chocolate to the mixture along with coffee, hot sauce, and salt; stir with your electric mixture for one minute or until all ingredients combined well.
8. Place the ice cream mixture in a freezer-safe container (with plastic film and lid over), and freeze for 6 hours or overnight.
9. Transfer frozen mixture to a bowl and beat with a mixer until smooth.
10. Repeat the process at least 5 times. This will to avoid ice cream crystallization.
11. If your ice cream gets too firm in the freezer, allow it to thaw at room temperature for 15-20 minutes before serving.

Mamey Sapote Ice Cream

Servings: 4

Preparation Time: 20 minutes

Nutrition Facts

Serving size: 1/4 of a recipe (4.2 ounces).

Percent daily values based on the Reference Daily Intake (RDI) for a 2000 calorie diet.

Nutrition information calculated from recipe ingredients.

Amount Per Serving

Calories 117.75

Calories From Fat (51%) 60.64

% Daily Value

Total Fat 6.93g 11%

Saturated Fat 4.18g 21%

Cholesterol 22.8mg 8%

Sodium 39.56mg 2%

Potassium 207.5mg 6%

Total Carbohydrates 13.35g 4%

Fiber 2.2g 9%

Sugar 9.66g

Protein 1.8g 4%

Ingredients

2 cup of mamey sapote pulp

2 cups whipped cream

1 tsp pure vanilla extract

1 cinnamon stick for decoration (optional)

2 fresh leaves of mint or spearmint

Instructions

1. Place the mamey pulp, whipped cream and vanilla extract in a mixing bowl.
2. Beat with an electric mixer until creamy and smooth.
3. Place the ice cream mixture in a freezer-safe container with a lid on; freeze for 6 hours.
4. Transfer frozen mixture to a bowl and beat with a mixer until smooth.
5. Repeat the process at least 5 times. This will to avoid ice cream crystallization.
6. Serve into chilled glasses with cinnamon sticks (optional) and mint leaves.

Author Note

Mamey sapote, is a species of tree native to Cuba and Central America, naturally from Cuba to southern Costa Rica, and Mexico.

A unique, tropical tree fruit with an interior texture that is both creamy and sweet, the vibrant salmon-colored flesh of the 'Pantin' mamey sapote is unlike anything most people have ever tasted. The flavor is a combination of sweet potato and pumpkin with undertones of almond, chocolate, honey, and vanilla.

Pineapple, Peppermint, and Mango Ice-cream

Servings: 10

Preparation Time: 20 minutes

Nutrition Facts

Serving size: 1/10 of a recipe (4.2 ounces).

Percent daily values based on the Reference Daily Intake (RDI) for a 2000 calorie diet.

Nutrition information calculated from recipe ingredients.

Amount Per Serving

Calories 121.84

Calories From Fat (1%) 1.42

% Daily Value

Total Fat 0.17g <1%

Saturated Fat 0.04g <1%

Cholesterol 0mg 0%

Sodium 124.32mg 5%

Potassium 134.73mg 4%

Total Carbohydrates 31.45g 10%

Fiber 1.2g 5%

Sugar 28.91g

Protein 0.58g 1%

Ingredients

3 cups pineapple, cored and cut into chunks

1 mango, cleaned and cut into pieces

1 cup brown sugar

1 cup water

1 lemon juice (freshly squeezed)

1/2 tsp salt

2 Tbs fresh peppermint finely chopped

1 Tbs fresh basil finely chopped

Instructions

1. Place the pineapple, mango, sugar, lemon juice and salt in your high-speed blender.
2. Blend 45 - 60 seconds on high or until all ingredients are combined well, and the sugar is dissolved.
3. Add the fresh mint and basil and blend for 30 - 45 seconds.
4. Place the mixture in a bowl and refrigerate for 2 hours.
5. Pour cold ice cream mix into an ice cream maker, turn on the machine, and churn according to manufacturer's directions, 20 to 25 minutes.
6. If you do not have an ice-cream maker; place the ice cream mixture in a freezer-safe container with a plastic lid over.
7. Freeze the ice cream in the freezer for at least 4 hours or overnight.
8. Transfer frozen mixture to a bowl and beat with a mixer until smooth.
9. Repeat the process at least 4 times to break up the ice crystals.
10. If your ice cream gets too firm in the freezer, allow it to thaw at room temperature for 15-20 minutes before serving.

Pulque Liquor Berries Ice cream

Servings: 8

Preparation Time: 20 minutes

Nutrition Facts

Serving size: 1/8 of a recipe (4.3 ounces).

Percent daily values based on the Reference Daily Intake (RDI) for a 2000 calorie diet.

Nutrition information calculated from recipe ingredients.

Amount Per Serving

Calories 255.44

Calories From Fat (15%) 38.19

% Daily Value

Total Fat 4.36g 7%

Saturated Fat 2.61g 13%

Cholesterol 14.25mg 5%

Sodium 25mg 1%

Potassium 73.14mg 2%

Total Carbohydrates 33.5g 11%

Fiber 1.62g 6%

Sugar 18.1g

Protein 1g 2%

Ingredients

3/4 cup raspberries (fresh or frozen)

3/4 cup blueberries (fresh or frozen)

3/4 cup blackberries (fresh or frozen)

1/2 cup bilberries (fresh or frozen)

1/2 cup granulated sugar or to taste

1 1/4 cup Pulque Liquor

2 1/2 cup whipped cream

3/4 cup chopped meringues

Instructions

1. In a deep bowl place the fruits; sprinkle fruit with a little sugar and pour the Pulque Liquor.
2. Refrigerate fruits in a sealed container for 4 hours.
3. Drain the fruits and keep the syrup in the refrigerator.
4. Beat the whipped cream and sugar with an electric mixer.
5. Add drained fruits and continue to beat on high speed.
6. Add crushed meringues and stir slightly.
7. Place the ice cream in the freezer in a container with lid; let it freeze for 6 hours or overnight.
8. Transfer frozen mixture to a bowl and beat with a mixer until smooth. Repeat the process at least 4 - 5 times.
9. Serve chilled with the fresh fruits and fruit syrup.

Author Notes

Pulque (occasionally referred to as agave wine) is an alcoholic beverage made from the fermented sap of the maguey (agave) plant. It is traditional to central Mexico, where it has been produced for millennia. It has the color of milk, somewhat viscous consistency and a sour yeast-like taste.

Rose Petals Sorbet

Servings: 6

Preparation Time: 15 minutes

Inactive Time: 4 hours

Nutrition Facts

Serving size: 1/6 of a recipe (4 ounces)

Percent daily values based on the Reference Daily Intake (RDI) for a 2000 calorie diet.

Nutrition information calculated from recipe ingredients.

Amount Per Serving

Calories 148.57

Calories From Fat (1%) 0.97

% Daily Value

Total Fat 0.12g <1%

Saturated Fat 0.03g <1%

Cholesterol 0mg 0%

Sodium 14.3mg <1%

Potassium 77.57mg 2%

Total Carbohydrates 37.45g 12%

Fiber 0.78g 3%

Sugar 35.48g

Protein 0.98g 2%

Ingredients

2 ounces rose petals, organic (pesticide free)

2 Tbsp of rose water for food use

1 cup of water

1 cup granulated sugar

2 1/2 Tbs of lemon juice, freshly squeezed

1 egg white from free-range chicken

1 Tbs of agave nectar

2 cups of ice cubes

Instructions

1. Place rose petals in a water and wash them well.
2. Remove the lower part of the petals and remove from the water on a kitchen paper.
3. When dry, chop them in small pieces.
4. Place sugar and water in a saucepan; bring to a boil over medium heat, stirring constantly.
5. Reduce heat to low and simmer for 2 minutes.
6. Remove from the heat and cool completely.
7. Place all ingredients in your high-speed power blender.
8. Blend for 2 minutes or until a homogenous mixture is achieved.
9. Place the mixture in a freezer-safe container allowing headspace for expansion; freeze for 4 hours. Serve in chilled glasses.

Açaí Berry Ice Cream

Servings: 4

Cooking Times

Preparation Time: 10 minutes

Nutrition Facts

Serving size: 1/4 of a recipe (5.3 ounces)

Percent daily values based on the Reference Daily Intake (RDI) for a 2000 calorie diet.

Nutrition information calculated from recipe ingredients.

Amount Per Serving

Calories 105.77

Calories From Fat (12%) 12.66

% Daily Value

Total Fat 1.3g 2%

Saturated Fat 0.28g 1%

Cholesterol 1.63mg <1%

Sodium 45.57mg 2%

Potassium 103.97mg 3%

Total Carbohydrates 14.93g 5%

Fiber 2g 8%

Sugar 10g

Protein 1.54g 3%

Ingredients

2 cup frozen acai berry pulp (or blueberries)

1/3 cup chopped strawberries

1/2 cup almond milk (or more if necessary)

1/3 cup of powdered milk

Sugar to taste

1/4 cup Açaí-blueberry vodka

Instruction

1. Place all ingredients in your high-speed blender or in a food processor.
2. Freeze the ice cream in the freezer for 4 hours.
3. Transfer frozen mixture to a bowl and beat with a mixer until smooth to break up the ice crystals. Repeat this process for 3-4 times.
4. Sprinkle with chopped nuts and serve.

Author Notes:

The acai berry is a fruit from a palm tree that is grown in the subtropic regions of Central and South America.

Anejo Cuatro Chocolate Ice Cream

Servings: 6

Cooking Times

Preparation Time: 20 minutes

Inactive Time: 4 hours

Nutrition Facts

Serving size: 1/6 of a recipe (3.8 ounces)

Percent daily values based on the Reference Daily Intake (RDI) for a 2000 calorie diet.

Nutrition information calculated from recipe ingredients.

Amount Per Serving

Calories 385.62

Calories From Fat (68%) 262.1

% Daily Value

Total Fat 29.45g 45%

Saturated Fat 17g 85%

Cholesterol 166.43mg 55%

Sodium 67.68mg 3%

Potassium 267mg 8%

Total Carbohydrates 23.57g 8%

Fiber 2.65g 11%

Sugar 16g

Protein 5.26g 11%

Ingredients

2 Tbs of butter

7 oz of dark bitter chocolate (preferably with 70% cocoa solids)

4 1/2 cups of whipped cream

1/2 cup powdered sugar

4 yolks organics

1 1/2 Tbs Anejo Cuatro Rum

Instructions

1. Melt the chocolate and butter in your microwave oven.
2. Combine melted chocolate, butter, and cream in a large mixing bowl.
3. In a separate bowl, whisk the sugar and yolks until a firm consistency.
4. Pour in a chocolate mixture and stir well until a homogeneous mixture is obtained.
5. Add the rum liqueur, stir well and let cool completely.
6. Place the ice cream mixture in a freezer-safe container (with plastic film and lid over) and freeze for 3 - 4 hours.
7. Transfer frozen mixture to a bowl and beat with a mixer until smooth.
8. Repeat the process at least 4 times. This will to avoid ice cream crystallization.
9. If your ice cream gets too firm in the freezer, allow it to thaw at room temperature for 15-20 minutes before serving. Enjoy!

Author Notes

Anejo Cuatro is a vibrant spirit with notes of honey, vanilla and oak spices, as well as a smooth palate that's rounded out by the inclusion of some five- and six-year-old rums.

Avocado Ice Cream with Spicy Chocolate Syrup

Servings: 8

Cooking Times

Preparation Time: 20 minutes

Inactive Time: 3 hours and 25 minutes

Nutrition Facts

Serving size: 1/8 of a recipe (5.2 ounces)

Percent daily values based on the Reference Daily Intake (RDI) for a 2000 calorie diet.

Nutrition information calculated from recipe ingredients.

Amount Per Serving

Calories 315.34

Calories From Fat (32%) 101.59

% Daily Value

Total Fat 12g 19%

Saturated Fat 2.63g 13%

Cholesterol 5.7mg 2%

Sodium 24.12mg 1%

Potassium 420.62mg 12%

Total Carbohydrates 53g 18%

Fiber 5.32g 21%

Sugar 46.27g

Protein 2.1g 4%

Ingredients

For the avocado ice cream

3 ripe avocados, pitted and sliced

1 cup of whipped cream, cold from the fridge

3/4 cup of sugar

1 lime juice

3 - 4 tsp of Tequila (optional)

Spicy chocolate syrup

1 cup of brown sugar

3/4 cup of water

1/4 cup of cocoa powder

1 pinch of ground cayenne or chili powder

Instructions

1. Open the avocados in half, remove the pit, peel them and put the pieces in your high-speed blender.
2. Add the lime juice, sugar, and very cold cream - but not frozen.
3. Add your favorite Tequila, and blend it until combined well.
4. Place the ice cream mixture in a freezer-safe container (with plastic film and lid over) and freeze for 2 - 3 hours.
5. To make the syrup, pour the water in a saucepan with the sugar and bring to boil about 5 minutes over high heat.
6. Let the syrup cool slightly, about 10-15 minutes.
7. Add the cocoa powder in a bowl, and add one tablespoon of the syrup.
8. Stir well until cocoa is combined well, without any lumps.
9. Pour syrup slowly in the cocoa powder, stirring all the time.
10. Add cayenne or chili powder to taste.
11. Remove the ice cream out of the freezer about 10 -15 minutes before serving so.
12. Decorate with the chocolate and chili syrup and serve.

Banana and Cacahuates Ice Cream

Servings: 8

Cooking Times

Preparation Time: 15 minutes

Inactive Time: 4 hours

Nutrition Facts

Serving size: 1/8 of a recipe (5 ounces)

Percent daily values based on the Reference Daily Intake (RDI) for a 2000 calorie diet.

Nutrition information calculated from recipe ingredients.

Amount Per Serving

Calories 257

Calories From Fat (51%) 130.15

% Daily Value

Total Fat 15.1g 23%

Saturated Fat 6.7g 34%

Cholesterol 26.21mg 9%

Sodium 31mg 1%

Potassium 328.1mg 9%

Total Carbohydrates 28.39g 9%

Fiber 2.54g 10%

Sugar 19.97g

Protein 5.11g 10%

Ingredients

3 frozen plantains, sliced

1 1/4 cup whole milk

1/3 cup sugar

1 tsp vanilla extract

1/2 cup cacahuates, finely chopped or ground

1/2 cup heavy cream

3 oz milk chocolate, cut into a piece

Instructions

1. Place the frozen plantain, milk, sugar, and vanilla in your high-speed blender. Pulse until smooth and creamy.
2. Transfer the mixture into mixing bowl and add the cacahuates. cream and chocolate.
3. Beat with an electric mixture until all ingredients combined well.
4. Put the ice-cream mixture in an ice cream machine and freeze it according to the manufacturer's instructions.
5. Place the ice cream mixture in a freezer-safe container (with plastic film and lid over) and freeze for at least 4 hours.
6. Let the ice cream at room temperature for 15 minutes before serving.

Fresita Strawberry Ice Cream

Servings: 8

Cooking Times

Total Time: 20 minutes

Nutrition Facts

Serving size: 1/8 of a recipe (5.6 ounces)

Percent daily values based on the Reference Daily Intake (RDI) for a 2000 calorie diet.

Nutrition information calculated from recipe ingredients.

Amount Per Serving

Calories 297.18

Calories From Fat (39%) 114.45

% Daily Value

Total Fat 13.12g 20%

Saturated Fat 7g 35%

Cholesterol 40.93mg 14%

Sodium 13mg <1%

Potassium 161.24mg 5%

Total Carbohydrates 43.74g 15%

Fiber 1.71g 7%

Sugar 41.29g

Protein 1.56g 3%

Instructions

4 cups strawberries, fresh or frozen

1 1/2 cups sugar

2 Tbsp water

2 cups half-and-half cream

1/4 cup Fresita wine

chopped walnuts for decoration

Instructions

1. Combine the strawberries, sugar, and water in a pan over medium heat; bring to a boil.
2. Reduce heat to low and simmer, uncovered until sugar is dissolved completely.
3. Stir in half-and-half and Fresita wine; stir well with a spatula.
4. Cover and refrigerate overnight.
5. Transfer frozen mixture to a bowl and beat with a mixer until smooth.
6. Repeat the process at least 5 times. This will to avoid ice cream crystallization.
7. Let the ice cream at room temperature for 15 minutes before serving.
8. Sprinkle with chopped walnuts, strawberries, add some whipped cream and serve.

Author Notes

Fresita ("Strawberries" in Spanish) is one of the worlds original sparkling wines that contains 100% natural strawberry pulp which helps this unique sweet sparkling obtain natural sweetness without added sugar or flavors.

Ice Cream de Chantilly and Raspberry

Servings: 8

Cooking Times

Preparation Time: 20 minutes

Inactive Time: 5 hours

Nutrition Facts

Serving size: 1/8 of a recipe (5.7 ounces)

Percent daily values based on the Reference Daily Intake (RDI) for a 2000 calorie diet.

Nutrition information calculated from recipe ingredients.

Amount Per Serving

Calories 212.53

Calories From Fat (51%) 108

% Daily Value

Total Fat 12g 18%

Saturated Fat 1.79g 9%

Cholesterol 0mg 0%

Sodium 968.74mg 40%

Potassium 117.16mg 3%

Total Carbohydrates 23.28g 8%

Fiber 2g 8%

Sugar 19.68g

Protein 3g 6%

Ingredients

1/2 cup of brown sugar

1/2 cup water

3 egg whites from free-range chickens

2 3/4 cups of milk cream

2 tsp of vanilla extract

2 cups of frozen raspberries

1/2 cup of palm sugar

Instructions

1. In a saucepan place the sugar and cover with water. Cook, stirring frequently until you get a clear syrup.
2. In a bowl, beat the egg whites with a help of an electric mixer until frothy.
3. Pour the syrup and continue to beat.
4. Add all remaining ingredients and beat for 45 - 60 seconds or until all ingredients combine well.
5. Place the ice cream mixture in a freezer-safe container (with plastic film and lid over) and freeze for 5 hours.
6. Transfer frozen mixture to a bowl and beat with a mixer until smooth.
7. Repeat the process at least 5 times. This will to avoid ice cream crystallization.
8. Let the ice cream at room temperature for 15 minutes before serving.
9. Decorate with meringue and raspberries and serve.

Mexican Horchata de Arroz Ice Cream

Servings: 6

Cooking Times

Preparation Time: 15 minutes

Inactive Time: 4 hours

Nutrition Facts

Serving size: 1/6 of a recipe (3.4 ounces)

Percent daily values based on the Reference Daily Intake (RDI) for a 2000 calorie diet.

Nutrition information calculated from recipe ingredients.

Amount Per Serving

Calories 239.79

Calories From Fat (72%) 172

% Daily Value

Total Fat 19.58g 30%

Saturated Fat 11.4g 57%

Cholesterol 181.47mg 60%

Sodium 22.73mg <1%

Potassium 119.19mg 3%

Total Carbohydrates 13.34g 4%

Fiber 0.51g 2%

Sugar 7.55g

Protein 3g 6%

Ingredients

1 frozen banana, cut into chunks

1/4 cup coconut sugar or to taste

3 Tbsp Mexican Horchata de Arroz

2 1/4 cups chilled heavy cream

4 egg yolks

Instructions

1. Place frozen banana and coconut sugar in your high-speed blender.
2. Blend for 45 - 60 seconds or until banana is completely mashed and coconut sugar combined well.
3. Pour Mexican Horchata de Arroz and beat for further 30 seconds.
4. In a separate bowl, beat the cream with help of an electric mixer (start on medium speed to prevent splattering, then speed up).
5. Once soft peaks start to form, you can add egg yolks and continue to beat until the cream reaches desired consistency.
6. Combine frozen banana mixture and cream mixture and beat for 30 - 45 seconds.
7. Place the ice cream mixture in a freezer-safe container and freeze it for at least 4 hours.
8. Let the ice cream at room temperature for 15 minutes before serving.

Author Notes

Horchatas, also called Aguas de horchata, is a popular type of drink in Mexico most commonly made with rice, but they can also be based on many other ingredients, from almonds to barley or oats to coconut—which is also delicious.

Nances and Apricot Ice Cream

Servings: 6

Cooking Times

Preparation Time: 10 minutes

Inactive Time: 4 hours

Nutrition Facts

Serving size: 1/6 of a recipe (5.9 ounces)

Percent daily values based on the Reference Daily Intake (RDI) for a 2000 calorie diet.

Nutrition information calculated from recipe ingredients.

Amount Per Serving

Calories 232.39

Calories From Fat (2%) 5.52

% Daily Value

Total Fat 0.66g 1%

Saturated Fat 0.02g <1%

Cholesterol 0mg 0%

Sodium 9mg <1%

Potassium 1021.82mg 29%

Total Carbohydrates 54g 20%

Fiber 7.51g 30%

Sugar 44.47g

Protein 2.97g 6%

Ingredients

1 lb fresh or frozen apricots pitted

1/4 lb nanches fruit, pitted

3 Tbs lemon juice

1 cup Greek yogurt

2 Tbs coconut sugar

Instructions

1. Combine apricots, nanches and lemon juice in a high-speed blender; blend for 45 seconds.
2. Add the Greek yogurt and coconut sugar, and continue to blend until smooth and creamy.
3. Place the ice cream mixture in a freezer-safe container and freeze for 4 hours.
4. Serve and enjoy!

Author Notes

Nance or Nanche is a tropical fruit from the Byronisma crahe treolia tree. The fruit is mostly grown in Southern Mexico through the Pacific side of Central America to Peru and Brazil. These fruits are sweet or sour in flavor, depending upon the cultivar.

Passion Fruit Ice Cream

Servings: 6

Cooking Times

Preparation Time: 25 minutes

Inactive Time: 6 hours and 15 minutes

Nutrition Facts

Serving size: 1/6 of a recipe (5.5 ounces)

Percent daily values based on the Reference Daily Intake (RDI) for a 2000 calorie diet.

Nutrition information calculated from recipe ingredients.

Amount Per Serving

Calories 378

Calories From Fat (52%) 196.43

% Daily Value

Total Fat 22.72g 35%

Saturated Fat 16.26g 81%

Cholesterol 54.34mg 18%

Sodium 28.51mg 1%

Potassium 202.9mg 6%

Total Carbohydrates 45.61g 15%

Fiber 0.04g <1%

Sugar 43.16g

Protein 1.68g 3%

Ingredients

2/3 cup glucose

1 glass of coconut milk

1 cup concentrated passion fruit juice

1 cup fresh cream

Syrup

1 cup sugar

1 cup water

1 cup passion fruit pulp

Instructions

Syrup

1. Place the sugar in a saucepan over the medium heat, and cook until forms a light caramel.
2. Pour water and the passion fruit pulp and boil until the caramel melts, without allowing it to thicken. It will avoid hardening after cooling.
3. Use a half of syrup to add to the ice cream and half to serve.

Ice Cream

1. Stir the glucose with the coconut milk until combined well.
2. Add the passion fruit juice and then the cream.
3. Whisk well and place to the freezer for about 6 hours.
4. Transfer frozen mixture to a bowl and beat with a mixer until smooth.
5. Repeat the process at least 5 times. This will to avoid ice cream crystallization. (on some point, add the half of syrup).
6. Let the ice cream at room temperature for 15 minutes before serving.
7. Serve with the syrup in chilled glasses.

Pineapple Sorbet Arbequina

Servings: 8

Cooking Times

Preparation Time: 20 minutes

Nutrition Facts

Serving size: 1/8 of a recipe (5.3 ounces)

Percent daily values based on the Reference Daily Intake (RDI) for a 2000 calorie diet.

Nutrition information calculated from recipe ingredients.

Amount Per Serving

Calories 222.41

Calories From Fat (21%) 45.89

% Daily Value

Total Fat 5.2g 8%

Saturated Fat 0.71g 4%

Cholesterol 0mg 0%

Sodium 74.23mg 3%

Potassium 124.75mg 4%

Total Carbohydrates 46.14g 15%

Fiber 1.65g 6%

Sugar 42.34g

Protein 0.61g 1%

Ingredients

1 pineapple, fresh and cut in pieces

1 1/4 cup of sugar

1 tsp fresh lime juice

3 Tbs of Extra Virgin Arbequina Oil for serving

Salt in flakes for servings

Instructions

1. Slice off the top green crown of pineapple with a sharp knife.
2. Cut about a half inch of the top.
3. Cut away the outer peel with a sharp knife from top to bottom.
4. Slice into bite-sized pieces and place in high-speed blender.
5. Add the sugar and lime juice; blend for 45 - 60 seconds or until the puree consistency is achieved.
6. Place the sorbet mixture in a freezer-safe container, and freeze it for 3 - 4 hours.
7. Serve in chilled glasses, sprinkle with little salt and Extra Virgin Arbequina oil.

Author Notes

Arbequina is a cultivar of olives. The fruit is highly aromatic, small, symmetrical and dark brown, with a rounded apex and a broad peduncular cavity. In Europe, it is mostly grown in Catalonia, Spain, but it is also grown in Aragon and Andalusia, as well as California, Mexico, Argentina, and Chile.

Ruddy Reposado Ice Cream

Servings: 6

Cooking Times

Preparation Time: 20 minutes

Inactive Time: 5 hours and 25 minutes

Nutrition Facts

Serving size: 1/6 of a recipe (3.4 ounces)

Percent daily values based on the Reference Daily Intake (RDI) for a 2000 calorie diet.

Nutrition information calculated from recipe ingredients.

Amount Per Serving

Calories 96.3

Calories From Fat (18%) 17.09

% Daily Value

Total Fat 1.95g 3%

Saturated Fat 1.21g 6%

Cholesterol 6.86mg 2%

Sodium 42.75mg 2%

Potassium 142.15mg 4%

Total Carbohydrates 12.17g 4%

Fiber 0.38g 2%

Sugar 11.25g

Protein 3g 6%

Ingredients

1 1/4 of frozen fruit mix (blueberries, cherries, currants ...)

1 1/4 cups yogurt

1/2 cup of whipped cream

2 Tbs agave syrup

1/4 cup Reposado Tequila

Instructions

1. Place the berry mixture with yogurt, cream, and syrup in your high-speed blender.
2. Blend until all ingredients are combined well.
3. Pour the Tequila and blend for 30 seconds.
4. Place the ice cream mixture in a freezer-safe container (with plastic film and lid over), and freeze for 4 hours.
5. Transfer frozen mixture to a bowl and beat with a mixer until smooth.
6. Repeat the process at least 5 times. This will to avoid ice cream crystallization.
7. Let the ice cream at room temperature for 15 minutes before serving.

Author Notes

The coloring of the tequila is clear and is usually 100% blue agave. Translated into English, Reposado Tequila means "restful", which implies that this type of tequila is aged or rested. Reposado Tequila is aged in white oak casks from 2 months to a year.

Sapodilla de Veracruz Ice Cream

Servings: 8

Cooking Times

Preparation Time: 15 minutes

Inactive Time: 6 hours

Nutrition Facts

Serving size: 1/8 of a recipe (6.1 ounces)

Percent daily values based on the Reference Daily Intake (RDI) for a 2000 calorie diet.

Nutrition information calculated from recipe ingredients.

Amount Per Serving

Calories 170.47

Calories From Fat (5%) 7.87

% Daily Value

Total Fat 0.94g 1%

Saturated Fat 0.16g <1%

Cholesterol 0mg 0%

Sodium 12.23mg <1%

Potassium 165.14mg 5%

Total Carbohydrates 42.1g 14%

Fiber 4.51g 18%

Sugar 24g

Protein 0.38g <1%

Ingredients

4 firm sapodilla

1 cup sugar

2 cups of water

1 glass of muscatel wine

Instructions

1. Peel sapodilla and mash to get a fine paste.
2. Place in a mixing bowl, and add sugar, water, and wine.
3. Blend with an electric mixer until all ingredients are combined well.
4. Place the ice cream mixture in a freezer-safe container (with plastic film and lid over).
5. Freeze for 6 hours.
6. Transfer frozen mixture to a bowl and beat with a mixer until smooth.
7. Repeat the process at least 5 times. This will to avoid ice cream crystallization.
8. Let the ice cream at room temperature for 15 minutes before serving.

Author Notes

Sapodilla, is a long-lived, evergreen tree native to southern Mexico, Central America and the Caribbean.

Tropical Sorbet

Mamoncillo

Servings: 6

Cooking Times

Preparation Time: 15 minutes

Inactive Time: 2 hours

Nutrition Facts

Serving size: 1/6 of a recipe (5.2 ounces)

Percent daily values based on the Reference Daily Intake (RDI) for a 2000 calorie diet.

Nutrition information calculated from recipe ingredients.

Amount Per Serving

Calories 116.56

Calories From Fat (6%) 7.37

% Daily Value

Total Fat 0.85g 1%

Saturated Fat 0.46g 2%

Cholesterol 2.45mg <1%

Sodium 29.86mg 1%

Potassium 331.1mg 9%

Total Carbohydrates 26.48g 9%

Fiber 1.67g 7%

Sugar 21.45g

Protein 3g 6%

Ingredients

1/2 cup mamoncillos pulp

2 frozen banana (ripe)

1 fresh pineapple cut into pieces

1 jar of natural yogurt

2 Tbs honey strained

Instructions

1. Whit a small and sharp knife clean the skin of Mamoncillo fruit and take out the pulp.
2. Place all other ingredients in a high-speed blender and blend until smooth.
3. Place the sorbet mixture in a freezer-safe container and freeze it for about 2 - 3 hours.
4. Serve in chilled glasses.

Author Notes

Mamoncillos (Melicoccus bijugatus) is native to Mexico, South and Central America, and the Caribbean and are also known as mamón, mamones, Spanish lime, quenepa, guinep, limoncillo, and a host of other names. They are traditionally eaten out of hand or used to make drinks, desserts, and jellies.

It tastes like citrus pitches, with a sour and sweet taste.

Tropical Mango and Cantaloupe Ice cream

Servings: 8

Cooking Times

Preparation Time: 15 minutes

Inactive Time: 7 hours

Nutrition Facts

Serving size: 1/8 of a recipe (6.5 ounces)

Percent daily values based on the Reference Daily Intake (RDI) for a 2000 calorie diet.

Nutrition information calculated from recipe ingredients.

Amount Per Serving

Calories 125.66

Calories From Fat (3%) 3.9

% Daily Value

Total Fat 0.46g <1%

Saturated Fat 0.11g <1%

Cholesterol 0mg 0%

Sodium 26.92mg 1%

Potassium 262.93mg 8%

Total Carbohydrates 30.17g 10%

Fiber 3g 8%

Sugar 28g

Protein 2.43g 5%

Ingredients

4 ripe mangoes, peeled and cut in cubes

2 wedges cantaloupe, cut in cubes

1 cup water

3 egg whites

1/2 cup cane sugar

Instructions

1. Place mango, cantaloupe, and water in your high-speed blender; blend until smooth.
2. In a bowl, beat the egg whites with cane sugar until firm. Add in mango/cantaloupe mixture and beat slightly.
3. Transfer the mixture to a container and freeze for 3 hours.
4. Pour cold ice cream mix into an ice cream maker, turn on the machine, and churn according to manufacturer's directions, 20 to 25 minutes.
5. Place in a freezer for 4 hours at least.
6. Let the ice cream at room temperature for 15-20 minutes before serving.

Vanilla and Gold Tequila Ice Cream

Servings: 6

Cooking Times

Preparation Time: 15 minutes

Inactive Time: 5 hours and 15 minutes

Nutrition Facts

Serving size: 1/6 of a recipe (3.5 ounces)

Percent daily values based on the Reference Daily Intake (RDI) for a 2000 calorie diet.

Nutrition information calculated from recipe ingredients.

Amount Per Serving

Calories 287.59

Calories From Fat (52%) 149.52

% Daily Value

Total Fat 17g 26%

Saturated Fat 9.97g 50%

Cholesterol 144.63mg 48%

Sodium 19.84mg <1%

Potassium 41.19mg 1%

Total Carbohydrates 29g 10%

Fiber 0g 0%

Sugar 28.52g

Protein 2.13g 4%

Ingredients

3 egg yolks

1 1/2 tsp vanilla sugar

6 oz sugar

1 cup water

2 cups cream

2 - 3 Tbsp Gold tequila

Instructions

1. Beat yolks and vanilla sugar.
2. Boil sugar and water in a saucepan until getting a clear syrup. Remove from heat and let cool completely,
3. Beat the cream until stiff and combine the egg yolk mixture.
4. Pour the syrup and Tequila and beat until all ingredients combined well.
5. Place the ice cream mixture in a freezer-safe container (with plastic film and lid over) and freeze for 4 - 5 hours.
6. It is recommended to stir several times your ice cream during freezing to avoid crystallization.
7. Serve and enjoy!

Author Notes

Gold tequila is made from agave and distilled into liquor, but it is more often a mix than 100 percent pure agave. The gold color can come either the tequila was aged in barrels that gave it a brownish hue or, more often, caramel or coloring was added to give it the golden hue.

PALETAS: Top 20 Mexican Ice Pops

The gastronomy of Mexico has a great diversity of typical dishes, for that reason, it was recognized, by UNESCO, as Intangible Heritage of Humanity. The basic and representative ingredients of Mexican dishes are corn, cilantro, chili, beans, piloncillo, nopal, and tomato.

Typical Mexican food: Los chilaquiles, El Taco, La torta ahogada, El pozole ...

Typical drinks of Mexico: Tequila is the flag drink of Mexico. It is made of agave by fermentation and distillation.

Aguas Frescas, Champurrado, Chandra

Typical sweets of Mexico: Chongos Zamoranos, Alegrías, Jamoncillo, Mexican Paletas

"Boozy" Apple - Cherry Ice Popsicles

Servings: 4

Preparation Time: 15 minutes

Nutrition Facts

Serving size: 1/4 of a recipe (3.5 ounces)

Percent daily values based on the Reference Daily Intake (RDI) for a 2000 calorie diet.

Nutrition information calculated from recipe ingredients.

Amount per Serving

Calories 93.67

Calories from Fat (7%) 6.37

% Daily Value

Total Fat 0.72g 1%

Saturated Fat 0.3g 1%

Cholesterol 2.73mg <1%

Sodium 57.15mg 2%

Potassium 69.76mg 2%

Total Carbohydrates 13.49g 4%

Fiber 0.64g 3%

Sugar 7.51g

Protein 1.16g 2%

Ingredients

4 Tbsp Rum

2 Tbsp of granulated sugar or to taste

2 lemons, freshly squeezed juice

3 ½ oz of green apple, peeled and sliced

2 Tbsp of candied cherries

3 Tbsp coconut water

Instructions

1. Stir rum with the sugar and a lemon juice.
2. In a processor or blender, process the peeled and cut apple along with the cherries and the lemon mixture.
3. Dump apple slices along with rum mixture, candied cherries, and coconut water in your blender, Blend until all ingredients are combined completely.
4. Pour the mixture into ice popsicles molds and insert the (preferable bamboo) sticks in every mold.
5. Freeze for several hours or overnight.
6. Remove the Popsicle from molds and serve.

Agua de Jamaica and Cantaloupe Ice Pops

Servings: 6

Preparation Time: 15 minutes

Nutrition Facts

Serving size: 1/6 of a recipe (4.3 ounces)

Percent daily values based on the Reference Daily Intake (RDI) for a 2000 calorie diet.

Nutrition information calculated from recipe ingredients.

Amount per Serving

Calories 53.4

Calories from Fat (2%) 1.28

% Daily Value

Total Fat 0.15g <1%

Saturated Fat 0.04g <1%

Cholesterol 0mg 0%

Sodium 13.46mg <1%

Potassium 230mg 7%

Total Carbohydrates 13.46g 4%

Fiber 0.71g 3%

Sugar 11.17g

Ingredients

2 ¼ cups cantaloupe chunks

¾ cup Agua de Jamaica

1 cup raw Brown Rice Syrup

3 Tbsp fresh lime juice

1 tsp lime zest

Instructions

1. Blend the cantaloupe chunks in your blender until achieve puree consistency.
2. Add Agua de Jamaica, Brown Rice Syrup, fresh lime juice, and lime zest; blend until smooth and combine well.
3. Pour the mixture into Popsicle molds.
4. Place Popsicles in a freeze for one hour.
5. Remove from the freeze and insert sticks in each mold.
6. Freeze for at least 4 hours or overnight.
7. Remove your goody pops from molds and serve.

Author Notes

"Agua de Jamaica which translates as "hibiscus water" is a typical agua fresca to accompany the mid-day meal in Mexico. It is sweet, tart, delicious and really refreshing all at the same time." (Source: Mexican Food Journal).

Cachaça Banana and Raspberry Popsicles

Servings: 8

Preparation Time: 15 minutes

Inactive Time: 6 hours

Nutrition Facts

Serving size: 1/8 of a recipe (4.7 ounces)

Percent daily values based on the Reference Daily Intake (RDI) for a 2000 calorie diet.

Nutrition information calculated from recipe ingredients.

Amount per Serving

Calories 134.92

Calories from Fat (1%) 1.32

% Daily Value

Total Fat 0.16g <1%

Saturated Fat 0.03g <1%

Cholesterol 0mg 0%

Sodium 12,66mg <1%

Potassium 132.91mg 4%

Total Carbohydrates 32.55g 11%

Fiber 1.11g 4%

Sugar 10.07g

Ingredients

2 frozen ripe bananas

1 1/2 cups of Greek yogurt

3 Tbsp agave syrup

3 - 4 Tbsp Cachaça*

3/4 cup fresh or frozen raspberry

Instructions

1. Place the banana in the high-speed blender until becomes creamy; set aside.
2. Add yogurt, agave syrup, and Cachaça and stir well; divide into two parts.
3. Blend the raspberries in a clean blender until melted.
4. Fill the Popsicle molds alternately with raspberry and white yogurt cream.
5. Place molds in a freezer for one hour.
6. At this point insert sticks into each mold.
7. Place popsicles in a freezer for about 6 hours or until completely frozen.
8. If you cannot remove the ice cream from the mold, dip the whole mold for 30 seconds in warm water, just enough to make the ice cream surface slightly melt and separate from the mold.
9. Ready! Serve!

Author Notes

The major difference between cachaça and rum is that rum is usually made from molasses, a by-product from refineries that boil the cane juice to extract as much sugar crystal as possible, while cachaça is made from fresh sugarcane juice that is fermented and distilled. It often tastes like a Rhum Agricole or Bianco tequila.

Cayenne Mango Popsicles

Servings: 8

Preparation Time: 15 minutes

Nutrition Facts

Serving size: 1/8 of a recipe (3.8 ounces)

Percent daily values based on the Reference Daily Intake (RDI) for a 2000 calorie diet.

Nutrition information calculated from recipe ingredients.

Amount per Serving

Calories 150.77

Calories from Fat (2%) 2.55

% Daily Value

Total Fat 0,3g <1%

Saturated Fat 0.07g <1%

Cholesterol 0mg 0%

Sodium 44.84mg 2%

Potassium 168.23mg 5%

Total Carbohydrates 38.57g 13%

Fiber 1.23g 5%

Sugar 37.09g

Ingredients

14 oz of mango pulp

1 mango cut in cubes

1 cup brown sugar

2 Tbsp lime juice freshly squeezed

Cayenne pepper to taste

1 pinch of salt

Instructions

1. In a blender, combine all ingredients from the list above.
2. Blend until brown sugar is completely dissolved.
3. Pour the mango mixture evenly into Popsicle molds or cups.
4. Place molds in a freezer, and freeze for 2 hours.
5. Remove Popsicle molds from the freezer, and insert sticks into each mold.
6. Freeze Popsicle molds for further 3 - 4 hours.
7. If you have a problem to un-mold your popsicles, just place molds under lukewarm water.
8. Serve.

Coconut and Chocolate Bounty Ice Pops

Servings: 6

Preparation Time: 15 minutes

Nutrition Facts

Serving size: 1/6 of a recipe (3.6 ounces)

Percent daily values based on the Reference Daily Intake (RDI) for a 2000 calorie diet.

Nutrition information calculated from recipe ingredients.

Amount per Serving

Calories 159.4

Calories from Fat (51%) 81.31

% Daily Value

Total Fat 9.25g 14%

Saturated Fat 6.31g 32%

Cholesterol 4.1mg 1%

Sodium 22.44mg <1%

Potassium 168.52mg 5%

Total Carbohydrates 13.25g 4%

Fiber 1.13g 5%

Sugar 9.64g

Protein 2.49g 5%

Ingredients

4 Tbsp of coconut flour

3/4 cup of coconut milk

1 cup of cow milk

Coconut sugar per taste (optional)

3 oz of dark chocolate (at least 60 - 69% of cacao solid)

3 Tbsp of dark rum

Instructions

1. Place in a deep ball all ingredients except chocolate; stir until combined well.
2. Pour the mixture into ice pop molds, add sticks and place in a freezer for 4 hours.
3. Melt dark chocolate in a microwave or over the steam.
4. Stir melted chocolate with dark rum.
5. Remove the ice pops from the freezer.
6. Pour melted chocolate over the frozen ice cream pops.
7. Place in a freeze until the chocolate is firm.
8. Serve.

Creamy Lemon Popsicles with Rosemary

Servings: 6

Preparation Time: 10 minutes

Nutrition Facts

Serving size: 1/6 of a recipe (5.3 ounces)

Percent daily values based on the Reference Daily Intake (RDI) for a 2000 calorie diet.

Nutrition information calculated from recipe ingredients.

Amount per Serving

Calories 401.4

Calories from Fat (39%) 154.77

% Daily Value

Total Fat 17.66g 27%

Saturated Fat 11g 55%

Cholesterol 66.58mg 22%

Sodium 132mg 6%

Potassium 429.48mg 12%

Total Carbohydrates 56.66g 19%

Fiber 1.77g 7%

Sugar 52.02g

Protein 8.52g 17%

Ingredients

1 can (15 oz) condensed milk

1 1/4 cups of cream

2 lemons, zest, and juice

1/2 tsp lemon extract

1- 2 sprigs of fresh rosemary

Instructions

1. Whisk the condensed milk and the milk cream in a bowl.
2. Add the zest, lemon juice, and lemon extract.
3. Beat with an electric mixer until a creamy consistency is obtained.
4. Place a piece of rosemary in each Popsicle mold and fill with lemon mixture.
5. Carefully insert sticks in each pops mold.
6. Store in freezer until the creamy lemon pops are firm.

Creme de Banana and Almonds Pops

Servings: 8

Preparation Time: 10 minutes

Nutrition Facts

Serving size: 1/8 of a recipe (3.7 ounces)

Percent daily values based on the Reference Daily Intake (RDI) for a 2000 calorie diet.

Nutrition information calculated from recipe ingredients.

Amount Per Serving

Calories 145,86

Calories From Fat (30%) 43,55

% Daily Value

Total Fat 5,16g 8%

Saturated Fat 0,72g 4%

Cholesterol 1,8mg <1%

Sodium 6,85mg <1%

Potassium 293,64mg 8%

Total Carbohydrates 22,36g 7%

Fiber 2,62g 10%

Sugar 11,25g

Protein 2,7g 5%

Ingredients

4 medium bananas cut in half

1 cup of strained yogurt

2 Tbsp Creme de banane (banana-flavored liqueur)

1/2 cup slivered almonds

Instructions

1. Line a glass or plastic container, (suitable for freezing), with the wax paper in a glass or plastic container.
2. Peel the bananas, and insert wooden sticks at the end of each banana.
3. Dip each banana in yogurt and sprinkle with slivered almonds.
4. Place bananas on a prepared container.
5. Place the container with bananas in the freezer for 4 hours or until completely firm.
6. Enjoy!

Author Notes

Creme de banane is a sweet, banana-flavored liqueur. It is mostly used in alcoholic drinks but also in cooking; it is an ingredient of various cocktails, ice creams, and desserts.

Dulce de Leche and Salted Coco Syrup Pops

Servings: 6

Preparation Time: 15 minutes

Nutrition Facts

Serving size: 1/6 of a recipe (3 ounces)

Percent daily values based on the Reference Daily Intake (RDI) for a 2000 calorie diet.

Nutrition information calculated from recipe ingredients.

Amount per Serving

Calories 252.44

Calories From Fat (55%) 139.1

% Daily Value

Total Fat 15.82g 24%

Saturated Fat 9.77g 49%

Cholesterol 58.57mg 20%

Sodium 72.27mg 3%

Potassium 77.64mg 2%

Total Carbohydrates 27.28g 9%

Fiber 0g 0%

Sugar 16.55g

Ingredients

1 cup of milk cream

1 cup of dulce de leche or caramel sauce

1 Tbsp Salted coconut syrup

1 tsp pure vanilla extract

Instructions

1. Beat the cream with a mixer (on medium) until creamy.
2. Place the cream in a freeze for one hour.
3. Add the dulce de leche, vanilla and "Salted Coconut Syrup", and continue beating until you get a firm consistency.
4. Pour the mixture in the palette - Popsicle molds, and freeze for one hour.
5. Remove Popsicle molds from freezer and insert wooden sticks in each mold.
6. Store in freezer for further 4 hours or until popsicles are completely firm.
7. Serve.

Author Notes

Caramel is made with a base of water, heavy whipping cream, sugar, and butter. Dulce de leche is a base of milk, sugar, and sometimes cinnamon. Dulce de leche is commonly made with condensed milk and simmered for hours, while caramel is a reduced mixture of water and sugar with the addition of HWC and butter.

Frozen Mexican Wine Popsicles

Servings: 6

Preparation Time: 20 minutes

Nutrition Facts

Serving size: 1/6 of a recipe (4.7 ounces)

Percent daily values based on the Reference Daily Intake (RDI) for a 2000 calorie diet.

Nutrition information calculated from recipe ingredients.

Amount per Serving

Calories 279.49

Calories from Fat (63%) 176.61

% Daily Value

Total Fat 19g 31%

Saturated Fat 11.27g 56%

Cholesterol 237.94mg 79%

Sodium 44mg 2%

Potassium 113mg 3%

Total Carbohydrates 20.38g 7%

Fiber 0g 0%

Sugar 18.83g

Protein 4.8g 10%

Ingredients

2 cups of cream

1 cup of milk

1/2 cup of sugar

6 egg yolks

1/2 cup of wine, such as the Albarolo or Calixa Rosado Grenache

Instructions

1. Cook the cream, milk, and sugar in a pot over low heat.
2. Stir and cook until sugar is dissolved.
3. Add egg yolks and stir for 4 - 5 minutes.
4. Place the cream/egg yolks mixture in a bowl and pour the wine; stir well.
5. Freeze the mixture for one hour.
6. Remove the ice cream mixture from the freezer and beat with the help of hand or electric mixer.
7. Ice cream is ready when a creamy consistency is obtained.
8. Add the mixture in Popsicle molds and insert the sticks.
9. Store in a freezer for several hours or until frozen. Serve.

Hot Cinnamon Cucumber Popsicles

Servings: 4

Preparation Time: 15 minutes

Nutrition Facts

Serving size: 1/4 of a recipe (4.1 ounces)

Percent daily values based on the Reference Daily Intake (RDI) for a 2000 calorie diet.

Nutrition information calculated from recipe ingredients.

Amount per Serving

Calories 51.33

Calories from Fat (12%) 6.4

% Daily Value

Total Fat 0.76g 1%

Saturated Fat 0.12g <1%

Cholesterol 0mg 0%

Sodium 140.34mg 6%

Potassium 218mg 6%

Total Carbohydrates 11.8g 4%

Fiber 2.41g 10%

Sugar 8.21g

Protein 1.14g 2%

Ingredients

3 cups of cucumber, peeled and de-seeded

1 cup of lemon juice

2 Tbsp of granulated sugar

2 Tbsp chili powder

1 tsp cinnamon

1 pinch of salt

Instructions

1. Peel the cucumber and remove the seeds.
2. Cut into medium cubes and place in the blender along with the lemon juice, sugar, chili, cinnamon, and salt.
3. Blend (without adding water) until smooth.
4. Sprinkle chili powder to the bottom of the molds, and pour the mixture in each Popsicle mold evenly.
5. Insert the sticks in every mold.
6. If using wooden sticks, freeze first 1 to 2 hours and then insert sticks.
7. Freeze 8 to 10 hours or until popsicles are completely firm.
8. To remove the popsicles easily, pass the mold through hot water for a few seconds.

Jicaleta and Tequila Liqueur Popsicles

Servings: 6

Preparation Time: 15 minutes

Nutrition Facts

Serving size: 1/6 of a recipe (5.3 ounces)

Percent daily values based on the Reference Daily Intake (RDI) for a 2000 calorie diet.

Nutrition information calculated from recipe ingredients.

Amount per Serving

Calories 57.82

Calories from Fat (2%) 1.34

% Daily Value

Total Fat 0.22g <1%

Saturated Fat 0.04g <1%

Cholesterol 0mg 0%

Sodium 104.25mg 4%

Potassium 219.2mg 6%

Total Carbohydrates 13.6g 5%

Fiber 7.11g 28%

Sugar 1.69g

Protein 1.24g 2%

Ingredients

1 medium jicama

2 lemons

1/4 cup Agavero Tequila Liqueur

1/4 cup chili powder

Salt to taste

Instructions

1. Peel the jicama fruit and cut into thick slices about 1 inch.
2. Insert the stick at the base of the jicama very carefully.
3. Squeeze lemon juice over jicama.
4. Pour Tequila Liqueur evenly over jicama.
5. Sprinkle each jicama stick with chili powder and salt.
6. Freeze for 6 hours or overnight. Serve.

Author Notes

Jicama resembles a giant turnip, but when cut and sliced are more like a crisper, albino cucumber. Inside, it looks like a potato, is crispy and juicy like a firm pear, but it tastes sweet and starchy like an apple. The best and most popular way to eat jicama is sliced and sprinkled with lime juice and chili powder.

Nutty Vanilla Popsicles

Servings: 10

Preparation Time: 10 minutes

Nutrition Facts

Serving size: 1/10 of a recipe (5.3 ounces)

Percent daily values based on the Reference Daily Intake (RDI) for a 2000 calorie diet.

Nutrition information calculated from recipe ingredients.

Amount per Serving

Calories 338.51

Calories from Fat (45%) 153

% Daily Value

Total Fat 17.93g 28%

Saturated Fat 5.18g 26%

Cholesterol 25.38mg 8%

Sodium 108mg 4%

Potassium 394.31mg 11%

Total Carbohydrates 37.27g 12%

Fiber 1.18g 5%

Sugar 35.51g

Protein 9.64g 19%

Ingredients

1 1/2 cup finely sliced walnuts

3 cups of whole milk

1 can (15 oz) condensed milk

1 Tbsp milk powder

2 tsp of pure vanilla extract

Instructions

1. Place the nuts, whole milk, condensed milk, milk powder and vanilla extract in your fast-speed blender.
2. Blend until ingredients are well corporate well.
3. Pour the mixture into Popsicle molds and carefully insert the wooden stick into the middle of each mold.
4. Freeze for at least 4 - 5 hours or until your ice popsicles are completely frozen.
5. Serve and enjoy!

Quirky Guanábana Popsicles

Servings: 8

Preparation Time: 10 minutes

Nutrition Facts

Serving size: 1/8 of a recipe (4.6 ounces)

Percent daily values based on the Reference Daily Intake (RDI) for a 2000 calorie diet.

Nutrition information calculated from recipe ingredients.

Amount per Serving

Calories 217.72

Calories from Fat (19%) 42

% Daily Value

Total Fat 4.77g 7%

Saturated Fat 3g 15%

Cholesterol 19.35mg 6%

Sodium 194/61mg 8%

Potassium 427.19mg 12%

Total Carbohydrates 37.6g 13%

Fiber 0.23g <1%

Sugar 37.17g

Protein 7g 14%

Ingredients

1 cup Guanábana - Soursop raw flesh without seeds

1/2 tsp pure vanilla extract

1/4 tsp table salt

1 can (15 oz) condensed milk

1 cup evaporated milk

1/2 cup coconut water

Instructions

1. Dump all ingredients above in your blender; blend until smooth and combine well.
2. Pour the mixture into popsicles molds and insert wooden sticks into each mold.
3. Place in freezer for several hours.
4. Serve and enjoy!

Author Notes

"Guanabana or soursop looks similar to jackfruit and tastes like a weird combo of strawberry, citrus, and banana. It's recommended that you avoid eating the seeds due to possible neurotoxins — however; the raw flesh of the fruit is a wonderful way to experience to the true essence of the soursop. Traditionally, soursop can be cut into segments and eaten raw." (Source: Why Wait to See the World?)

Rumy Mamey Sapote Popsicles

Servings: 8

Preparation Time: 15 minutes

Nutrition Facts

Serving size: 1/8 of a recipe (4.5 ounces)

Percent daily values based on the Reference Daily Intake (RDI) for a 2000 calorie diet.

Nutrition information calculated from recipe ingredients.

Amount per Serving

Calories 124.42

Calories from Fat (8%) 10.41

% Daily Value

Total Fat 1.2g 2%

Saturated Fat 0.68g 3%

Cholesterol 3.68mg 1%

Sodium 54.26mg 2%

Potassium 185.18mg 5%

Total Carbohydrates 24g 8%

Fiber 1.5g 6%

Sugar 17.65g

Protein 3.48g 7%

Ingredients

2 cups or mamey sapote pulp

2 Tbsp dark rum

2 cups of plain yogurt

1/2 cup of brown sugar or to taste

Instructions

1. Cut the mamey fruit and extract the pulp.
2. Put it in the blender and add dark rum, yogurt, and brown sugar.
3. Blend until sugar is dissolved and all ingredients are combined well.
4. Pour the mamay fruit mix into a Popsicle mold and freeze for one hour.
5. Remove from the freezer and insert wooden sticks in every Popsicle mold.
6. Freeze for further 4 hours.
7. Serve.

Author Notes

"Mamey sapote, is a species of tree native to Cuba and Central America, naturally ranging from southern Cuba to southern Costa Rica, plus Mexico. The flavor is a combination of sweet potato and pumpkin with undertones of almond, chocolate, honey, and vanilla." (Source: Slow Food USA)

Sour Guanabana Blueberry Popsicles

Servings: 10

Preparation Time: 15 minutes

Nutrition Facts

Serving size: 1/10 of a recipe (3.7 ounces)

Percent daily values based on the Reference Daily Intake (RDI) for a 2000 calorie diet.

Nutrition information calculated from recipe ingredients.

Amount per Serving

Calories 62.05

Calories from Fat (28%) 17.34

% Daily Value

Total Fat 2.07g 3%

Saturated Fat 0.21g 1%

Cholesterol 0.37mg <1%

Sodium 34.43mg 1%

Potassium 152.13mg 4%

Total Carbohydrates 10.48g 3%

Fiber 1.14g 5%

Sugar 8.4g

Protein 1.47g 3%

Ingredients

2 cups of blueberries

2 cups of blueberry juice

1/4 cup of yogurt

2 Tbsp of lime juice

2 Tbsp of Soursop (Graviola Fruit) Butter

1 pinch of salt

Instructions

1. Place blueberries and blueberry juice in a pot and bring to boil over strong heat; stir frequently.
2. Reduce the heat and simmer for two minutes stirring occasionally.
3. Remove it from heat and let it cool completely.
4. Pour cold blueberry syrup in your high-speed blender.
5. Add all remaining ingredients from the list above; blend until all ingredients are combined well.
6. Pour the mixture into Popsicle molds and insert the sticks.
7. Place in a freezer overnight.
8. Serve.

Sparkling Champagne Berry Popsicles

Servings: 4

Preparation Time: 10 minutes

Nutrition Facts

Serving size: 1/4 of a recipe (3.8 ounces)

Percent daily values based on the Reference Daily Intake (RDI) for a 2000 calorie diet.

Nutrition information calculated from recipe ingredients.

Amount per Serving

Calories 51.68

Calories from Fat (7%) 3.74

% Daily Value

Total Fat 0.45g <1%

Saturated Fat 0.02g <1%

Cholesterol 0mg 0%

Sodium 1.17mg <1%

Potassium 146.17mg 4%

Total Carbohydrates 9.61g 3%

Fiber 4.21g 17%

Sugar 4.32g

Protein 0.99g 2%

Ingredients

2 cups of champagne

8 strawberries, sliced

8 raspberries, sliced

8 blackberries, sliced

Fresh mint leaves finely chopped (optional)

Instructions

1. Wash and cut fruits in thick slices.
2. Place fruit slices in each Popsicle mold.
3. On this point, add fresh chopped mint if using.
4. Pour the champagne into each mold, and insert sticks.
5. Freeze for 3 to 4 hours.
6. Ready! Serve and enjoy!

Spicy Mango and Chamoy Popsicles

Servings: 6

Preparation Time: 15 minutes

Nutrition Facts

Serving size: 1/6 of a recipe (3.4 ounces)

Percent daily values based on the Reference Daily Intake (RDI) for a 2000 calorie diet.

Nutrition information calculated from recipe ingredients.

Amount per Serving

Calories 97.3

Calories from Fat (2%) 2.29

% Daily Value

Total Fat 0.27g <1%

Saturated Fat 0.06g <1%

Cholesterol 0mg 0%

Sodium 60.52mg 3%

Potassium 103mg 3%

Total Carbohydrates 24.81g 8%

Fiber 1.03g 4%

Sugar 23.63g

Protein 0.52g 1%

Ingredients

1 cup of mango

2 Tbsp of lemon juice

1/2 cup of sugar or Stevia granulated sweetener

1/4 cup of water

1 tsp chili powder

1/2 cup of mango cut into cubes

1/4 cup of chamoy

Instructions

1. Add mango, lemon juice, sugar or stevia granulated sweetener, water, and chili powder in a fast-speed blender; blend until combined well.
2. Add mango cubes, and a little chamoy in popsicles molds and fill with the mango-lemon mixture.
3. Freeze mango popsicles for one hour.
4. Remove popsicles from the freezer and insert sticks into each mold.
5. Freeze the Popsicle mold for further 3 - 4.
6. Unmold and enjoy.

Author Notes

"Chamoy refers to a variety of savory sauces and condiments in Mexican cuisine made from pickled fruit. Chamoy may range from a liquid to a paste consistency, and typically its flavor is salty, sweet, sour, and spiced with chillis." (Source: Wikipedia)

Strawberry and Xtabentún Popsicles

Servings: 6

Preparation Time: 15 minutes

Nutrition Facts

Serving size: 1/6 of a recipe (3.9 ounces)

Percent daily values based on the Reference Daily Intake (RDI) for a 2000 calorie diet.

Nutrition information calculated from recipe ingredients.

Amount per Serving

Calories 102.15

Calories from Fat (17%) 17.56

% Daily Value

Total Fat 2.05g 3%

Saturated Fat 1.53g 8%

Cholesterol 7.04mg 2%

Sodium 46.86mg 2%

Potassium 167.58mg 5%

Total Carbohydrates 15.25g 5%

Fiber 0.03g <1%

Sugar 11.27g

Protein 3.44g 7%

Ingredients

1 lb fresh strawberry

Juice of one lemon

2 Tbsp coconut milk

2 Tbsp condensed milk

Filling

1 can (15 oz) of condensed milk

2 Tbsp Xtabentún - anise liqueur

Instructions

1. Blend strawberries, lemon juice, coconut milk and condensed milk in a fast-speed blender.
2. In a small bowl, stir the condensed milk and anise liqueur
3. Fill the strawberry mixture in a half of each pops mold.
4. Then, pour the anise liqueur mixture up to 3/4 of each mold.
5. In the end, fill remaining strawberry mixture in each mold.
6. Place in freezer for one hour.
7. Remove your ice pops from the freezer and insert stick in each mold.
8. Freeze for 3 - 4 hours and serve.

Author Notes

"Xtabentún is an anise liqueur made in Mexico's Yucatán region from anise seed, and fermented honey produced by honey bees from the nectar of xtabentún flowers." (Source: Wikipedia)

Stunt Popsicles with Passion Fruit Cream

Servings: 10

Preparation Time: 20 minutes

Nutrition Facts

Serving size: 1/10 of a recipe (4.8 ounces)

Percent daily values based on the Reference Daily Intake (RDI) for a 2000 calorie diet.

Nutrition information calculated from recipe ingredients.

Amount per Serving

Calories 354.56

Calories from Fat (34%) 122.16

% Daily Value

Total Fat 14g 22%

Saturated Fat 8.55g 43%

Cholesterol 43.59mg 15%

Sodium 127.13mg 5%

Potassium 413.79mg 12%

Total Carbohydrates 47.05g 17%

Fiber 0.3g 1%

Sugar 41.05g

Protein 7.44g 15%

Ingredients

1 can (11 oz) of condensed milk

1 Tbsp Mexican whipping buttercream (or butter)

3 Tbsp of grated dark chocolate

1/2 tsp of cinnamon

1 cup of passion fruit pulp

1 can (11 oz) of condensed milk

1 cup of sour cream

Instructions

1. Cook condensed milk, whipping buttercream, cinnamon, and grated chocolate in a saucepan over low heat; stir all the time.
2. Cook for about 5 minutes or until all ingredients melt and creamy.
3. Transfer the condensed milk mixture into a container and let cool.
4. In a meantime, place in a blender passion fruit pulp, condensed milk, and sour cream.
5. Process in the blender and then add this mixture in half of Popsicle molds.
6. Freeze the popsicles for one hour.
7. Remove the popsicles from the freezer and pour cold condensed milk mixture in each mold.
8. Insert the sticks in each mold and freeze for further 4 hours or overnight.
9. Ready! Enjoy!

Tarragon Avocado Popsicles

Servings: 6

Preparation Time: 10 minutes

Nutrition Facts

Serving size: 1/6 of a recipe (5.4 ounces)

Percent daily values based on the Reference Daily Intake (RDI) for a 2000 calorie diet.

Nutrition information calculated from recipe ingredients.

Amount per Serving

Calories 166.85

Calories from Fat (76%) 127.21

% Daily Value

Total Fat 15.19g 23%

Saturated Fat 6.77g 34%

Cholesterol 0mg 0%

Sodium 18.31mg <1%

Potassium 391.46mg 11%

Total Carbohydrates 9.33g 3%

Fiber 4g 16%

Sugar 0.73g

Protein 1.77g 4%

Ingredients

2 avocados

2 lemons, juice

2 Tbsp granulated sugar or sweetener to taste

1 1/4 cup of water

3 cup of coconut milk

20 fresh tarragon leaves finely chopped

Instructions

1. Place avocado, lemon juice, granulated sugar or sweetener, water, coconut milk and chopped tarragon in your blender.
2. Blend until avocado/lemon mix is creamy in texture.
3. Pour the mixture into Popsicle molds and insert sticks in every mold.
4. Freeze for overnight until completely frozen.
5. Serve.

Made in the USA
Las Vegas, NV
16 August 2023